Auditing community participation

An assessment handbook

Danny Burns and Marilyn Taylor

The POLICY PRESS

First published in Great Britain in July 2000 by

The Policy Press
34 Tyndall's Park Road
Bristol BS8 1PY
UK

Tel no   +44 (0)117 954 6800
Fax no   +44 (0)117 973 7308
E-mail   tpp@bristol.ac.uk
http://www.policypress.org.uk

Reprinted 2001

Published for the Joseph Rowntree Foundation by The Policy Press

ISBN 1 86134 271 3

Danny Burns is Lecturer at the School for Policy Studies, University of Bristol, and **Marilyn Taylor** is Professor of Social Policy at the Department of Community Studies, University of Brighton.

The **Joseph Rowntree Foundation** has supported this project as part of its programme of research and innovative development projects, which it hopes will be of value to policy makers, practitioners and service users. The facts presented and views expressed in this report are, however, those of the authors and not necessarily those of the Foundation.

Cover design by Qube Design Associates, Bristol
Front cover: right photograph kindly supplied by Cadmium Systems Limited; left photograph kindly supplied by www.johnbirdsall.co.uk
Printed in Great Britain by Hobbs the Printers Ltd, Southampton

Contents

Acknowledgements	iv
Introduction	1
Why audit community participation?	1
Why should communities participate?	1
Is audit relevant to community participation?	2
Developing an audit tool	3
Designing audit	3
What to measure	3
How to measure it	5
What the measures offer	6
Who does the audit?	6
The audit tools	7
The audit process	7
How the tables are organised	8
Using the tables	8
1 Mapping the history and pattern of participation	11
2 The quality of participation strategies adopted by partners and partnerships	19
3 The capacity of partner organisations to support community participation	35
4 The capacity within communities to participate effectively	45
5 Impact assessments	53
Postscript	60
References and further reading	61

Acknowledgements

Many of the ideas that have gone into this audit framework have come from over a decade of work with community activists and professionals. All of these people deserve some credit.

In relation to this specific project we would like to thank the following people:

Community activists from Lewisham, Kings Cross and Birmingham for initial discussions which helped us to create the framework.

Birmingham Community Forum for participating in focus groups which helped us to refine the frameworks (a special thanks to Barry Toon for organising these).

Officers from Birmingham City Council who talked through the draft framework with us.

Members of the Goldsmiths research team who worked alongside us on this project – Marj Mayo, Michael Keith, Jean Anastacio, Ben Gidley, Ute Kowarzik and Lorraine Hart.

Alison Gilchrist, Frances Heywood, Lorraine Hart for detailed comment on the final draft.

Paul Burton for his thoughtful comments on the usability of the tables.

Roger Tarling for an important discussion on the use of scales.

Members of the Joseph Rowntree Foundation Project Advisory Board:

Bob Colenut

Howard Simmons, Director of Leisure, London Borough of Hounslow

Phillipa Holland, Government Office for the West-Midlands

Gary Craig, Policy Studies Research Centre, Humberside University

John Gaventa, Development Studies, University of Sussex

Alan Barr, Scottish Community Development Centre

Christine Bainton, Community Forum

Mandy Wilson, COGS

Nisa Ahmed

John Low our JRF project manager – for enabling the project to get off the ground, and supporting us through the process.

Karen Bowler for spending considerable time on the design, enabling the publication to be accessible and usable.

Introduction

Why audit community participation?

Partnership is a central theme of government policy today. There is also an increasing commitment to community participation and community-led partnerships. But partnership and community involvement are not new; and despite successive regeneration initiatives, all the evidence suggests that, in the past, there has been a considerable gap between rhetoric and reality. Even now communities and their representatives often feel marginalised – on the edges of power. There have been a number of reasons for this, but briefly, the evidence suggests that:

- the 'rules of the game' are set from above;
- the cultures and structures of public sector partners are not compatible with effective community involvement;
- communities themselves do not have the organisational capacity and resources for effective involvement.

Some of the lessons from the past are being learnt through the New Deal for Communities and the more recent rounds of the Single Regeneration Budget. They are also enshrined in the proposed National Strategy for Neighbourhood Renewal, where neighbourhood residents are seen as crucial.

> The involvement and leadership of local people is vital to turning round deprived neighbourhoods and helping them to thrive. (SEU, 2000, para 4.10./2)

However, there is still a lot of variation in the practice of partnerships around the country and across the different departments of public authorities. What can be done to ensure that public bodies and others involved in partnerships give more priority to community involvement? How can we be sure that the rhetoric of partnership with communities is translated into effective practice?

One thing that public bodies and partnerships do take seriously is the need to account for public money through financial audit. Over the years the need to account for public money has influenced the ways that public bodies are structured and the systems and procedures that they set up. It has also influenced the way that partnerships are designed and run. If a similarly rigorous account had to be given of the measures taken to encourage community involvement, would this ensure that public authorities and partnerships were structured in ways that facilitated genuine participation and took community issues and views on board?

Why should communities participate?

One of the reasons communities are marginalised is because partners are not convinced of the value of participation. It is worth, therefore, rehearsing the arguments for community participation.

> **Why is community participation essential?**
>
> • Community definitions of need, problems and solutions are different from those put forward by service planners and providers.
>
> • Community knowledge is an important resource, and widens the pool of experience and expertise that regeneration and renewal strategies can draw on.
>
> • Community participation gives local residents the opportunity to develop skills and networks that they need to address social exclusion.
>
> • Active participation of local residents is essential to improved democratic and service accountability.
>
> • Central government requires community participation in regeneration and neighbourhood renewal strategies.

Is audit relevant to community participation?

At first glance, the idea of applying audit mechanisms to community participation may seem fraught with difficulties.

First, public bodies and partnerships already have to deal with ever-growing demands for regulation, recording and monitoring. Is further regulation and audit the way to encourage more effective practice in community participation? Or does it simply add to a system of carrots and sticks that inhibit effective action and take time away from the front line? It is clear from research that bureaucracy acts as a barrier to participation. Would a community participation audit stifle the very processes it is meant to encourage?

Second, the culture of audit appears to run counter to many of the principles that underpin community participation. Audit is based on rules and measures. It is task oriented and specific, often based on quantitative measures imposed from the outside. Community participation, on the other hand, needs to be based on trust. It is about processes and learning – building quality in rather than testing it out. Neighbourhood renewal and regeneration are complex processes – there are no simple solutions. Effective partnerships with communities, some argue, need to be flexible and to have the room to evolve rather than being based on the tried and the tested. (For a discussion of the evolutionary nature of partnerships, see Pratt et al, 1999.)

Audit	Community participation
Rules	Trust
Risk averse	Flexible
Quantitative	Qualitative
Task driven	Value driven
External control	Autonomy

However, Ed Mayo of the New Economics Foundation (Mayo, 1996) suggests that audit has the following strengths. It is:

• comprehensive
• regular
• comparative
• externally validated
• transparent.

These strengths have been recognised in the growing movement over recent years to introduce social audits into public and private organisations. Social audit is used to check how far organisations are achieving objectives other than the financial bottom line, such as equal opportunities and environmental sustainability.

In adapting traditional audit mechanisms to new objectives, social audits have developed other characteristics. Social audit aims to:

• draw on many perspectives, not just one;
• reflect local circumstances – for example, political context, organisational capacity;
• encourage enquiry and learning;
• be peer driven rather than top-down;
• be qualitative rather than just quantitative.

Approached in this way, audit can be used positively to **facilitate** learning and dialogue, rather than as a stick to beat those who have not yet learnt how to perform effectively or jump through the right hoops. It can be done in partnership rather than imposed from the top down.

However, developing this approach to auditing community participation does throw up a number of challenges.

First, ways of auditing would need to be found to reflect the **diversity** within communities, the time it takes to involve these diverse communities and the dynamics of involvement. There are likely to be waves or **cycles of involvement**, according to the stage of partnership and the significance of the issues it is addressing. Second, ways of auditing would also need to reflect the different starting points and pressures on different partners. In particular, they would need to take account of the **complexity** of accountability within partnerships – the fact that different partners are accountable to different bodies and constituencies for different things. Third, they would need to understand and find ways of expressing the **intangibles** of community involvement and to find **simple measures for complex processes** – measures that would be meaningful to all the partners without reducing participation to a lowest common denominator.

It is important that a participation audit should not be another set of measures imposed on communities and their partners from above. Simplistic indicators set from outside the local situation encourage people to find ways of avoiding them. If community participation is to be audited, the tools that are used need to be something that all partners in participating communities can use and that can be jointly owned.

Developing an audit tool

A study funded by the Joseph Rowntree Foundation and carried out by researchers at Goldsmiths College, University of London, has been evaluating community involvement in previous regeneration schemes – particularly City Challenge and Single Regeneration Budget Partnerships. Although there was variation between the case study partnerships that were studied, the research found that residents still felt

that the power in partnerships lay elsewhere and that they were on the margins of partnership.

As part of this study, researchers from the Universities of Brighton and Bristol explored the possibility of developing a tool for auditing community involvement. They began by carrying out three group discussions with residents and community representatives currently involved in the partnerships being studied by the Goldsmiths team. The purpose of these discussions was to find out what community participants in partnerships thought were important indicators of community participation. The researchers then drew on these discussions and on previous research to design an initial set of audit tools. They then ran two further groups – one with community representatives, one with local authority officers – to find out how useful they thought the tools might be. The attached set of 'audit tools' is the product of that process. While designed for regeneration partnerships, the tools could be used for other initiatives that require public bodies to engage with communities.

Designing audit

The design of the audit tools needed to address four key questions:

- What to measure?
- How to measure it?
- What the measures offer to those engaged in partnerships?
- Who should do the measuring?

Building on the earlier discussion, we were looking for something that would ask simple but meaningful questions, that would be easy to use, that would be useful and relevant to all the stakeholders and that would have credibility.

What to measure

The audit tools are grouped under five headings. The initial section is designed to establish the context within which participation is being introduced.

The next three sections ask what needs to be in place for community participation to be effective. These questions are based on the three problem areas that we identified at the beginning of this introduction, and aim to establish whether

1 Mapping the history and pattern of participation

Key question	Indicator
A What is the range and level of local community activity?	Partners have a clear picture of the range and levels of community participation which already exist.
B What communities are there within the localities covered by the partnership?	Partners have a clear picture of the different communities that may wish to participate.
C What local barriers are there to participation?	Partners are aware of the barriers to participation and have considered how they might be addressed.

2 The quality of participation strategies adopted by partners and partnerships

Key question	Indicator
1a Who or what has determined the rules of the partnership?	Local communities are involved as equal partners in setting the rules and agendas for the partnership.
1b What is the balance of power within the partnership?	Communities have as much power and influence as other key stakeholders.
2a Where in the process are communities involved?	Communities are involved in all aspects of the partnership process.
2b How much influence/control do communities have?	Communities are given the opportunity to have effective influence and control.
3a What investment is made in developing and sustaining community participation?	Partnerships invest significant time, money and resources in developing participation.
3b How strong is the leadership within partnerships and partner organisations?	There is long-term, committed and skilled leadership for participation within the partnership and partner organisations.
4 Does the community participation strategy allow for a variety of 'ways in'?	(a) A variety of different approaches to participation are being tried. (b) Attention is paid to strengthening all forms of community participation.

3 The capacity within partner organisations to support community participation

5 Can decisions be taken at neighbourhood level?	Decisions can be taken at a level that local communities can influence.
6 Do decision-making structures allow for local diversity?	Neighbourhoods/localities can be different from one another.
7 Are services 'joined-up'?	Partner organisations can deliver integrated solutions to problems.
8 Are service structures compatible with community participation?	Service structures, boundaries and timetables are compatible with neighbourhood and community structures, boundaries and timetables

4 The capacity within communities to participate effectively

9 How accessible are local meetings?	Local community groups are accessible to potential members.
10 Are community groups able to run in an effective and inclusive way?	Local groups work in an effective, open and inclusive way.
11 How do groups ensure that their representatives are accountable?	Representatives are accountable and have the power to make decisions.

5 Impact assessments

12 How effective is participatory decision making?	(a) Issues of importance to the community get on to agendas. (b) Decisions made by the community are implemented.
13 What are the outcomes of participation?	Outcomes result from participation that would not have happened if participation had not occured.
14 Who benefits from participation?	(a) Opportunities are provided for all sections of the community to participate. (b) Participation benefits all sections of the community.

adequate systems and processes are in place to ensure that the participation can be achieved. They cover:

- The participation strategies adopted by partnerships and the 'rules of the game'.
- The structure, culture and management of partners' own organisations and the extent to which these allow them to engage with and respond to communities (the 'capacity' within partners).
- The organisational capacity within communities.

These three areas form the core of the audit tools. They are followed by a short section on outcomes.

In each area, there are a small number of questions that the audit needs to address. Each question is followed by a short paragraph explaining why it is important and stating the indicator that the response would provide. These are summarised below.

There are many more issues that could be audited under each heading, but it is important to start with a process that is manageable. The attached tools are intended as a starting point only, drawing attention to some of the key issues. The tools will be piloted and will need to be customised for local use, drawing on the ideas and priorities of local communities and other partners.

How to measure it

For each of these questions, there is a 'tool' or 'appraisal exercise'. There are three main types of audit tool:

1. Baseline mapping exercises to establish the context within which participation is being introduced.
2. Checklists of:
   - activities or approaches that contribute to effective community involvement;
   - questions that need to be asked if community involvement is to be effective.
3. Scales to help stakeholders think through the quality and extent of the participation activities that they are putting in place.

Some of the questions require **statements of fact**, which can be used to make assessments of participation at different points in the development of a partnership, but many (especially the checklists and scales) require **subjective judgements**, because they are difficult to measure in any objective way. These judgements may vary between partners and communities.

A fourth type of tool, which applies only to outcomes, is a 'decision trail' to track:

- how and whether selected items raised by communities get onto the decision-making agenda;
- how these items are eventually decided – and by whom;
- how the decision was reported back to the various partner organisations and communities;
- what happened to the decision en route to implementation;
- if and how it was implemented and by whom;
- how it was monitored.

The decision trail can be used in two ways. It can start with an item that a local community puts on the partnership agenda which can be tracked through the decision-making process to see whether it is implemented or blocked. Using a decision trail would be like putting dye in the system and seeing where it flows through and where it gets blocked. Alternatively, the decision trail can start with a decision that has clearly come out of the partnership and track back to where it came from. This is equally important: it is important for partners to be prepared to ditch cherished top-down plans that local communities do not see as a priority; it is also important that communities as well as partners are creating the agenda for partnership.

What the measures offer

The tools are designed to:

- identify the elements that make for effective partnership with communities – the issues that agencies and communities in partnerships need to think about;
- identify the options that are available for effective community participation;
- identify where there is room for improvement;
- identify where there is already good practice to build on;
- offer external validation.

They give participants in partnership some criteria with which to engage in debate, but they can be customised to the local situation. Their purpose is to act as an aid to analysis, debate and learning within the partnership. The intention is that they should give partnerships the tools to:

- develop a strategy;
- assess their progress over time;
- compare different experiences and perceptions within the partnership;
- learn together about what works and what does not;
- benchmark against other partnerships.

For example, those tools that require subjective judgements provide an opportunity to compare and contrast the perceptions of different stakeholders. Thus, asking 'What is the balance of power within the partnership?' will show whether different stakeholders have different views on this subject. It will also provide the basis for discussion about the evidence on which these views are based. The extent to which different stakeholders make different judgements may change over time, with more agreement as and when power is shared more widely. It would also be useful to repeat the preliminary mapping exercises later in the process to assess whether participation in the partnership has had any impact on community participation more generally.

Who does the audit?

The exercises can be used as a self-assessment tool, but we suggest that they will be most effective if there is an outside facilitator, especially if they are to be used for external validation. The most effective way of providing this facilitation would be through peer audit, using teams of experienced community representatives and community professionals from other regeneration areas. These teams would be trained in the use of these tools, perhaps with the support of researchers or consultants with relevant experience. Such teams could form a Community Participation Audit Commission, which would develop the tools further to ensure that they promote good practice and support those who are committed to making participation work. Some consideration would need to be given to how to fund such teams, but if regeneration funders are serious about community participation, an investment in audit might be a good way of ensuring that the rhetoric becomes reality.

The audit tools

The audit process

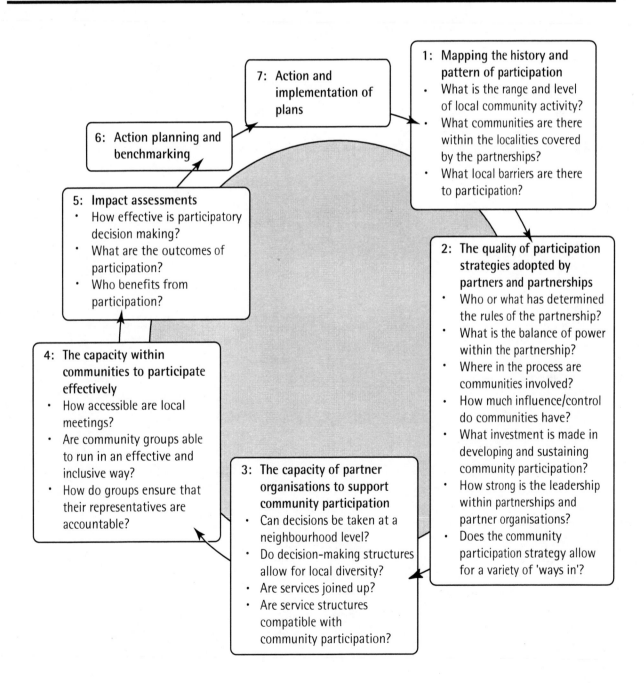

7: Action and implementation of plans

1: Mapping the history and pattern of participation
- What is the range and level of local community activity?
- What communities are there within the localities covered by the partnerships?
- What local barriers are there to participation?

6: Action planning and benchmarking

5: Impact assessments
- How effective is participatory decision making?
- What are the outcomes of participation?
- Who benefits from participation?

2: The quality of participation strategies adopted by partners and partnerships
- Who or what has determined the rules of the partnership?
- What is the balance of power within the partnership?
- Where in the process are communities involved?
- How much influence/control do communities have?
- What investment is made in developing and sustaining community participation?
- How strong is the leadership within partnerships and partner organisations?
- Does the community participation strategy allow for a variety of 'ways in'?

4: The capacity within communities to participate effectively
- How accessible are local meetings?
- Are community groups able to run in an effective and inclusive way?
- How do groups ensure that their representatives are accountable?

3: The capacity of partner organisations to support community participation
- Can decisions be taken at a neighbourhood level?
- Do decision-making structures allow for local diversity?
- Are services joined up?
- Are service structures compatible with community participation?

How the tables are organised

The categories

As indicated in the accompanying text, the tables are grouped into five categories.

- Mapping the **context** for participation.
- The **quality of participation strategies** adopted by partners and partnerships.
- The **capacity of partner organisations** to support community participation.
- The **capacity within communities** to participate effectively.
- **Impact** assessments.

The title

This indicates the general area that the table covers.

Type of table

On the table is an indication of whether the table represents a:

- mapping exercise;
- checklist;
- scale;
- decision trail.

Below the title are three boxes. The **Explanation** box gives the reasons why this table is important to participation. The **Indicator** box summarises the key evidence which should be sought be those carrying out the audit. The **Exercise instructions** box explains how to use the table.

Table

The tables are constructed to help you to think through what it is that the partnership or partnership organisation is doing. We have selected the categories from our experience of studying participation over many years; they have been refined through focus groups with community activists. However, you may wish to add categories before any audit is carried out. The table has two columns: in the first column is a description of a level or type of activity; in the second column is an explanation or example of it to help illustrate the type of thing you need to look for.

Number

On each table there is a number: this is for ease of reference. It also relates to the checklist of indicators. Where a table is given a number and a letter such as 2a and 2b, the two tables should be used together. The Exercise instructions paragraph explains how this should be done.

Using the tables

It is important that you should not be constrained by the categories we have suggested. If you feel that some of the descriptions are not appropriate to your circumstances, take them out. If you feel that there are important things missing, put them in. You may also want to construct completely new tables. This could take place either at the baseline stage or as a result of the monitoring and assessment process.

We do, however, suggest that you follow the order that we have suggested. In other words it makes sense to carry out a baseline mapping first (1), then assess the quality of participation (2), and the capacity of partners (3) and communities (4) to meet the demands of community participation. Carrying out an assessment of the impact of participation should come last in the audit cycle (5). Following this the cycle starts again with an action plan, which includes both benchmarks and targets against which the next round of assessment will be measured (6) and finally (7) an action/implementation stage.

There are different ways in which you can record the information.

Brain storming

Start with a blank sheet of paper and put down everything you can think of that relates to a particular issue or indicator. Do not worry what order it is in, or what sense it makes. When this exercise is completed see if it fits easily into the categories in the table. If it does not, add new ones or take some away.

Web diagrams

Many people find it easier to see the relationship between things by drawing web diagrams: these start with the issue or key question at the centre and work outwards (see diagram below). For example, you might start with the words 'local communities', then list those communities, map all of the participation initiatives which relate to each community.

Work directly with the tables

You may choose to work directly with the headings in the tables. For example when you are working with Table 4 you might choose to list all of the different types of forums, all of the groups that are funded and so on. Against each of these things you might want to record other information such as the amount of funding they receive.

Maps

You may find it helpful to trace the geographical boundaries of the area that you are considering and plot your information onto an actual map.

Evidence

Web diagram

Wherever possible evidence should be provided to support the views expressed in the audit. This might take the form of documents, hard facts, examples or anecdotes. This evidence should be kept alongside any summary material which relates to the tables.

The important thing is that it is stored in a way in which it can be retrieved and made sense of so that progress can be monitored.

Comparison

All of these exercises should be used to enable detailed comparisons between different groups involved in the audit. It will, for example, be important to compare local councillors' views about barriers to participation with those of people from different local communities.

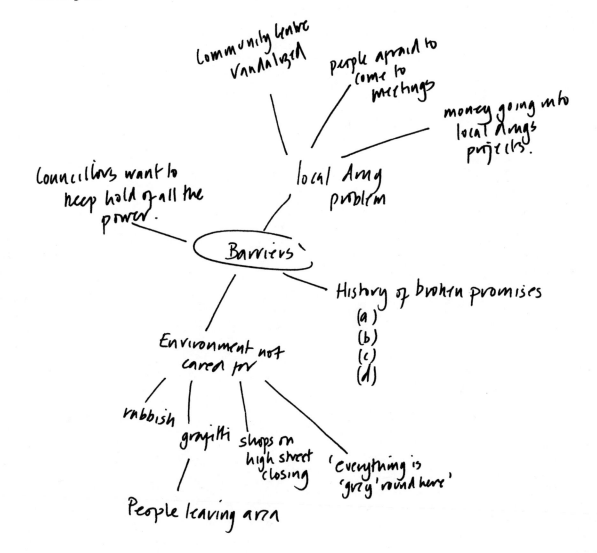

Mapping the history and pattern of participation

What is the range and level of local community activity?

Explanation

Participation strategies often focus on the creation of structures and decision-making forums without thinking about how to strengthen communities. Active neighbourhoods with high levels of participation in the wider community are likely to produce more representatives to sit on committees than inactive neighbourhoods dominated by a few unrepresentative individuals. Furthermore, effective community participation will build on what is already there. Community participation should be seen as the foundation of participation in institutional decision making.

Key indicator

Partners have a clear picture of the range and levels of community participation which already exist.

Exercise instructions

As far as is possible all the different types of community activities that take place within neighbourhoods should be mapped under the following catagories.

Unless they are particularly relevant to your area try *not* to use the examples below. They are there for illustration.

Table A	Baseline mapping
Category	**Example** *Try not to limit yourself to the examples given*
Individual contributions to community	Sweeping closes, keeping garden nice, volunteering
Individual involvement in community activities	Local football teams, bowling, luncheon clubs etc
Informal mutual aid	Community protection, childcare exchange, neighbouring
Organised mutual aid	LETS, Credit Unions, Neighbourhood watch
Participation in local networks and associations	Tenants' and residents' groups, community associations etc

Decision making in community institutions	School PTAs or governing bodies, churches, community centres etc
Decision making on public committees and partnership boards	Area committees, partnership boards etc

Notes

What communities are there within the localities covered by the partnership?

Explanation

Most public institutions treat 'the community' as a single entity. It is not – it is comprised of many different overlapping communities. Even where community participation strategies are successful, some communities may be privileged and others excluded. It is important that the voices of all communities are heard.

Key indicator

Partners have a clear picture of the different communities that may wish to participate.

Exercise instructions

All communities that are present in the area should be identified. The categories below can be used as a starting point for identifying them.

Unless they are particularly relevant to your area try *not* to use the examples below. They are there for illustration.

Table B	Baseline mapping
Category	**Example** *Try not to limit yourself to the examples given*
Service users	For example, school parents, housing tenants, park users, residents of older people's homes, and so on
Ethnic and religious communities	There may be a strong mix of religions and backgrounds within a locality
Economic communities	Working-class people have different needs to middle-class people. Unemployed people have different needs again
Sub-communities	Asian women, for example, may have very different views from Asian men
Age-based groups	Very often children and older people have no involvement in decision-making processes

B: What communities are there within the localities covered by the partnership?

Geographical communities	Different neighbourhoods have different needs
Communities of interest	For example dog owners
Communities of identity	For example lesbian women and gay men
Workplace communities	Student nurses or workers at a car plant may be an important presence in a locality. Small businesses represent a different sort of workplace community
'Outcast' communities	For example, homeless people, ex-offenders, Travellers

Notes

What local barriers are there to participation?

Explanation

There are a whole range of factors – not all of which relate to the participation process itself – which will have a significant impact on participation.

Key indicator

Partners are aware of the barriers to participation and have considered how they might be addressed.

Exercise instructions

Local factors which may inhibit participation should be identified. Map the issues that are relevant to the neighbourhoods within your partnership area. Try to list as may as possible – big and small. These can then be monitored over time. Action plans can be drawn up and these can also be monitored. *Note:* It is important to focus on *local* barriers – things on which partners, partnerships and communities can have an impact.

The examples listed below are just a few of the many hundreds of barriers that could have an effect on participation in your area – you will inevitably find many more.

Table C	Baseline mapping
Example	**Explanation**
Violence, drug use, anti-social behaviour/harassment	May deter people from going to meetings because they fear going out
Perceptions that nothing changes	People may have low expectations of change
Lack of care for and pride in the community	May lead people not to care enough about their environment to participate
Racism and 'not in my backyard' attitudes	Can set different sections of the community against each other and lead some to be excluded
Domination of meetings by individuals or groups	Often some people feel excluded from participating because of a few dominant individuals
Poor experiences of participation in the past	People may have been involved in previous participation exercises where nothing happened

Notes

The quality of participation strategies adopted by partners and partnerships

Two

1a

Who or what has determined the rules of the partnership?

Explanation

This table identifies how the partnership was set up and, in particular, who the key players were in structuring it. The way in which the decision-making process is constructed at the outset will have a huge impact on who has power and how it is used.

Key indicator

Local communities are involved as equal partners in setting the rules and agenda for the partnership.

Exercise instructions

Participants should be asked who they think has control over the different aspects of the partnership listed under the category headings below. This can be done in conjunction with Table 1b.

Table 1a	Baseline mapping
Category	**Explanation**
The structure of the partnership	Who decided on the way the partnership was structured – its constitution, what sub-committees and working groups it has, and so on?
Level of representation and who is represented on the main partnership board	Who decided who should be represented, how many representatives different partners should have and how local communities should be represented?
The structure and proceedings of meetings	Often meetings are run according to local authority custom and practice with little opportunity for communities to suggest changes.
The strategic agenda	Who decided what the overall aims and objectives of the partnership are?

Targets, monitoring and performance criteria	Often these are imposed by central government and interpreted through local authorities as accountable bodies. Communities rarely get to devise bottom-up criteria for monitoring and evaluation
The definition of the local community	Who defined the geographical area to be covered?
Defining community needs	These should be based on a needs appraisal exercise which fully involves the community in design, collection and analysis

Notes

1b

What is the balance of power within the partnership?

Explanation

It is important to identify where real power lies. For example, in some areas political parties are the dominant force. Decisions may be made before they even reach the partnership board. Consideration will need to be given as to how the balance of power can be equalised over the long term in context of the above. This might include, for example, the construction of jointly agreed partnership plans.

Note: This is not a broad question about where power lies within the local system. It is specifically about decision making in the partnership.

Key indicator

Communities have as much power and influence as other key stakeholders.

Exercise instructions

This is a general question about the partnership, and participants should rank the different players. Evidence (even in the form of anecdotes) should be produced to support views expressed. One way of identifying where the balance of power lies is to ask people who or what they feel accountable to.

This list may also be used as a prompt in answering some of the questions in 1a.

Table 1b		Checklist
Checklist		**Examples**
Funders	☐	This could include Europe, central government, the RDA, the National Lottery
The accountable body	☐	There may be a lead agency that has more power in the partnership than other partners
Councillors	☐	
Regulatory agencies	☐	The Housing Corporation, Audit Commission
Professionals or officers	☐	
Behind the scenes networks	☐	This could include political parties or religious groupings and so on.

Business interests ☐

Community representatives ☐   Having equal representation on the board does not necessarily mean equal power. There may be some community representatives who are seen to have more power than others

Other ☐

Notes

2a

Where in the process are communities involved?

Explanation

Partnerships may offer communities different levels of participation in different decision-making arenas. These need to be benchmarked. Table 1a will have established who set the rules at the outset. This exercise will audit ongoing decision making in the partnership.

Key indicator

Communities are involved in all aspects of the partnership process.

Exercise instructions

These should be ranked on a scale of 1-9 using scale 2b, asking, 'What is the level of participation?'

Table 2a		Checklist
Checklist		**Explanation**
Policy making	☐	
Strategic planning	☐	This includes budgeting decisions
Commissioning or deciding who gets funded	☐	This includes project appraisal
Budgetary control	☐	
Managing partnership staff	☐	Including, appointing, disciplining, appraising and training staff
Recruitment and disciplinary matters	☐	
Identifying performance indicators and targets	☐	
Monitoring and scrutiny	☐	
Planning individual projects	☐	
Managing individual projects	☐	

Notes

How much influence/control do communities have?

Explanation

It is important to be clear about what level of participation is offered in each decision-making arena. This does not mean that control (2) is better than limited delegation (4), but it may be. It is important to recognise, for example, that control and limited delegation have quite different implications for participation.

This scale is based on Arnstein's ladder of participation and the adapted framework of Burns et al (1994).

Key indicator

Communities are given the opportunity to have effective influence and control.

Exercise instructions

This scale should be used wherever it is suggested that the levels of participation are benchmarked.

All arenas of participation should be identified and attributed with a level of participation according to the scale below.

Table 2b   Scale

Position on scale	Explanation
Ownership	Community have ownership of all assets – there are no conditions which have to be met
Control	Communities have control over all activities, but only within conditions laid out in contractual arrangements
Substantial delegation	Partner organisations give substantial control over decision making to communities
Limited delegation	Partner organisations give limited control over decision making to communities
Advisory input	Communities have a formal advisory role
Genuine consultation	Communities are properly and genuinely consulted

High quality information	7	Communities are given high quality information
Consultation controlled by decision makers	8	Communities are consulted, but only on options which have been carefully constructed by those with the power
Lip-service only	9	Despite the rhetoric participation amounts to nothing

Notes

3a

What investment is made in developing and sustaining community participation?

Explanation

Community participation does not just happen – it needs a strategy, resources, commitment, time and a planned approach. It also requires attention to capacity building in partner agencies as well as communities.

Key indicator

Partnerships invest significant time, money and resources in developing participation.

Exercise instructions

Careful consideratiuon should be taken of levels, type and quality of investment. This will be important for comparison year by year.

Table 3a   Checklist

Checklist		Explanation
Is there a strategy for community participation?	☐	Is there (a) evidence of a strategy, (b) evidence of its implementation?
Is there a budget?	☐	How much is allocated (what proportion of total spend does it comprise)? The sister report to this publications suggests that 10% is an appropriate figure
Are specialist workers employed?	☐	(a) Are they free to act on behalf of communities? (b) Are they on time-limited or long-term contracts?
Is there any investment to support community activity?	☐	This could include buildings, facilities, newsletters or new technology
Is there any investment in community umbrella or intermediary bodies to support involvement?	☐	Communities need the infrastructure to support involvement and representation
Is there strong leadership to support community participation?	☐	To help determine this you may wish to use Table 3b

3a: What investment is made in developing and sustaining community participation?

Is there a strategy for capacity building within partner organisations? ☐ Too often capacity building is applied to local communities only. Effective participation requires skills throughout partner agencies as well

Are there opportunities for joint learning and training? ☐ Joint training can be a very powerful way of breaking down barriers

Notes

3b

How strong is the leadership within partnerships and partner organisations?

Explanation

Many community participation strategies have collapsed because they have not had sustained political leadership. This is critical in situations requiring organisational change – even more so where powerful interests will be resistant to that change. Weak political leadership is likely to consign a participation strategy to the dustbin before it has even got off the ground.

Key indicator

There is long-term, committed and skilled leadership for participation within the partnership and partner organisations.

Exercise instructions

Assess the commitment of both partners and the partnership on the scale below. Community groups may also wish to use this scale to help think through whether *they* have effective leadership.

Table 3b   Scale

Position on scale	Explanation
No leadership	Participation is espoused but is not formulated into any meaningful policy
Tokenistic leadership (rhetoric)	Despite policy statements there is no real commitment
Instrumental leadership	Participation is not seen as desirable in itself. It is championed only for as long as it helps to achieve other objectives (for example, when trying to achieve a housing stock transfer)
Resistant leadership	Institutions often bring in resistant managers to manage radical change processes in order to bring them on board. Evidence shows that this seldom works
Committed but marginalised leadership	Commitment to change may be strong, but it may not be driven from the centre of power

Short-term leadership from the centre of power	Initiatives can lose momentum if committed leaders delegate to others
Sustained leadership from the center of power	Initiatives need sustained leadership of this sort to be successful

Notes

4

Does the community participation strategy allow for a variety of 'ways in'?

Explanation

A strategy that invests in the creation of neighbourhood forums without building social capital within the community may quickly discover that few people get involved and those that do are not representative of their communities. Research evidence suggests that participation across a wide range of community activity is likely to strengthen participation in institutional decision making – increasing the number of representatives and ensuring their accountability.

There are many ways in which institutions can support community participation. These include bringing community representatives into organisational decision-making processes, local neighbourhood forums and voluntary and community sector funding strategies.

Key indicator

(a) A variety of different approaches to participation are being tried.
(b) Attention is paid to strengthening all forms of community development as an indirect route to strengthening community participation.

Exercise instructions

Using the checklist below, partnerships and partners should establish which arenas of community participation their strategy addresses.

Table 4   Checklist

Checklist		Explanation
Delegated powers to decision-making and consultative forums	☐	Including neighbourhood forums, area committees, community councils
Voluntary sector funding	☐	Funding the voluntary sector can help to build vibrant local communities rich with social capital. These are the foundations of participation strategies
Funding of community organisations	☐	Funding of tenants' associations, support to luncheon clubs, and so on . This may be a double-edged sword as local authorities often use the threat of withdrawing funding as a way of keeping groups in line

4: Does the community participation strategy allow for a variety of 'ways in'?

Community development	☐	Tenant participation officers, community development workers. This would also include network development work
Support to informal mutual aid and self-help activities	☐	For example, funding LETS officers, or supporting good neighbouring schemes
Support to community business	☐	This could include advice, subsidised premises, access to professional services etc
Provision of facilities and buildings	☐	These could range from community centres to football pitches or places for education
Capacity building and technical assistance	☐	This might include skills training (such as committee skills), funding of independent advice (on, for example, stock transfer)

Notes

The capacity of partner organisations to support community participation

Three

5

Can decisions be taken at a neighbourhood level?

Explanation

Community participation is based on the idea that local people or key stakeholders can have an impact on issues that specifically affect them. For this to be possible local managers and/or local councillors need to have delegated authority to respond to local community opinions.

Key indicator

Decisions can be taken at a level that local communities can influence.

Exercise instructions

Using the scale below, an assessment should be made of the extent to which decisions are made at the front line by each partner organisation.

Table 5   Scale

Position on scale	Explanation
Centralised policy and implementation	Everything is determined by the centre
Delegated implementation	Policy can be implemented locally but not locally determined
Limited discretionary powers	Some discretion is given to local officers
Delegated decision making	Within broad policy parameters, local officers have autonomous powers to act
Devolved decision making	Policy over issues which have only a local impact is devolved
Devolved planning	All departments have devolved decision making enabling the construction of integrated community plans

Notes

6

Do decision-making structures allow for local diversity?

Explanation

The extent to which institutions are prepared to allow diversity is a strong indicator of the extent to which local participation is real. If communities are able to construct their own plans and identify their own priorities, these will inevitably be different from community to community (see Baseline Table B).

Key indicator

Neighbourhoods/localities can be different from one another.

Exercise instructions

Using the scale below, an assessment should be made of the degree to which diversity is allowed by each partner organisation.

Note: This type of assessment should not only be used to assess service diversity across neighbourhoods, but also things such as community group constitutions.

Table 6	Scale
Position on scale	**Explanation**
One uniform product	Everybody gets the same (one meal for all)
Set menu	Diversity is reflected in pre-set choices. Different neighbourhoods or groups may choose different options, but they have the same options available to them. (You can select from a preset menu)
Variations within strict limits	Some locally determined variation is possible but strict limits are applied from the centre to ensure an appearance of equity. (You can ask for carrots instead of broccoli with your meal)
Innovation allowed but centrally approved	This is most often likely to be in a pilot project situation where the organisation sees the variation as a forerunner to a uniform programme. (Local menus approved by the centre)

Local flexibility	Flexibility to depart from the norm is allowed, but the norm still represents the dominant force within the organisation
Local diversity	Diversity is encouraged, and a culture of difference is supported. (Any meal can be asked for)

Notes

7

Are services joined up?

Explanation

The degree to which partners and partnerships are able to integrate their services is fundamental. If services are not integrated, community governance will be limited to tasks such as managing a local housing estate or governing a local school. Local people see issues as being connected and will want to develop holistic solutions to problems. If institutions do not have the capacity to integrate their own services, community planning will not be achievable. For communities, making decisions across service boundaries at a local level is a meaningless exercise if institutions do not have the capacity to deliver on them.

Key indicator

Partner organisations can deliver integrated solutions to problems.

Exercise instructions

Each partner organisation should be assessed on the scale below. Assessment should be made:
(a) in relation to individual projects;
(b) overall.

Table 7	Scale
Position on scale	Explanation
Hostility to contact	Other departments and agencies are seen as a threat
Non-cooperation	Agencies often have tunnel vision and see themselves as the centre of the universe. They are often unable to see the benefits of cooperation
Information exchange	Information is exchanged but it is usually carefully vetted
Coordination	Avoidance of duplication or clashes
Cooperation	Contributing to one another's projects
Collaboration	Partnerships, working with others
Joint project working	Single team leader, colocation of staff

Joint planning

Cross-boundary planning

Joint decision making

Collective decisions over staffing

Integrated services

Pooled budgets and resources

Notes

8

Are service structures compatible with community participation?

Explanation

One of the most common weaknesses of participation strategies is the lack of administrative coordination that underpins them. This takes a number of forms, as shown below.

Key indicator

Service structures, boundaries and timetables are compatible with neighbourhood and community structures, boundaries and timetables.

Exercise instructions

The checklist below should be used to assess both partner organisations and partnerships.

Table 8   Checklist

Checklist		Explanation
Decision-making structures which mirror community structures	☐	Do the partners have committees which parallel neighbourhood forums?
Effective relationship between representative and participatory democratic structures	☐	For example, do councilors support community decision making?
Participative decision-making structures of partners effectively coordinated	☐	Large numbers of competing and overlapping forums can sap the energy of a few activists and create inefficient duplication
Neighbourhood decision making effectively linked to service decision making	☐	Is the organisation structured to allow geographical, service, user and corporate decision-making processes to run along side each other?
Geographical boundaries aligned	☐	Without this it is very difficult for communities to get accurate information to assess and monitor services and budgets for their area
Decision-making timetables aligned	☐	If timetables are not effectively coordinated, community involvement is rendered meaningless

Notes

The capacity within communities to participate effectively

Four

9

How accessible are local meetings?

Explanation

Community participation often centres on local meetings. Effort needs to be made to attract people to meetings and to ensure that they feel that it is worth coming back.

Key indicator

Local community groups are accessible to potential members.

Exercise instructions

Community meetings should be identified. They might be assessed through visits by community activists in another region.

Note: This checklist should only be seen as a list of basics. Without the addressing the other issues in this audit, they may have little or no long-term impact.

Table 9   Checklist

Checklist		Explanation
Adequate notice of meetings	☐	People need time to arrange childcare etc
Childcare available	☐	This could take the form of crèches or childcare allowances and so on
Warm meeting rooms	☐	People are put off by cold meeting rooms and do not come back
Accessible buildings	☐	Consideration should be given to siting meetings on bus routes, to making sure there is good disabled access and so on
Meetings on community territory	☐	More people are likely to come to meetings if the meeting feels as if it is 'their's'
Refreshments	☐	This should be culturally appropriate
Varied meeting times	☐	People have different commitments; sometimes it will be appropriate to hold the same meeting twice at different times

Meeting arranged in a circle	☐	Traditional meetings which are arranged with a top table do not encourage people to engage in discussion with each other
Interpretation and translation (where necessary)	☐	This could include signing
Technical aids such as hearing loops	☐	
Simple information and not too much of it	☐	50-page agendas in complicated language are still not uncommon
Accessible language	☐	Make sure that jargon is kept to a minimum
Problem-solving format	☐	It is better for community activists to work through issues and come up with solutions than to be presented with options
Time for strategic planning	☐	Community decision-making meetings can quickly get drawn into examining small detail; they rarely spend time thinking about what people want for the whole neighbourhood
Separate sessions to air individual complaints	☐	Too often meetings get clogged up with individuals' complaints about their own problems – these need to be aired but not during the main meeting time
Agendas constructed by tenants and residents	☐	Too often tenants and residents are there simply to comment on reports and issues presented by councils or partnership officers
Expenses for attendance	☐	Many people cannot attend meetings because they have to take time off work or get childcare
Provision of transport where appropriate	☐	Transport does not have to be provided formally; often facilitating informal arrangements help people to get to meetings that they would otherwise not be able to get to

Notes

10

Are community groups able to run in an effective and inclusive way?

Explanation

There are a whole range of problems associated with community groups. For example, groups may be dominated by a few individuals who are not acting in the interest of the groups as a whole. Because these people often have control over the information it is easy for them to disguise their negative behaviour.

Key indicator

Local groups work in an effective, open and inclusive way.

Exercise instructions

Using the scale below, groups should seek evidence of good meeting skills and mechanisms.

Table 10   Checklist

Checklist	Explanation
Is the group able to retain the participation of those who come to meetings?	Many groups fail to retain interested newcomers because they are put off meetings, by the established members of the group. Evidence could include the ratio of those who attend once to those who return over a period of time
Does the group have the diversity and experience to work effectively and to represent communities?	Evidence of diversity of backgrounds and of skills should be sought
Do group members have the information that they need?	Specialist professional knowledge, knowledge of local governance structures, equal opportunities and so on
Does the group have the skills and mechanisms to deal with negative group behaviour?	Cynicism and/or domination of groups by those who shout the loudest will often put others off. Conflict is inevitable but groups need support in handling and mediating difference. Mechanisms could include limits on speaking times; skills needed include mediation skills

Are there mechanisms for ensuring turnover and bringing new people on board?	These might include time limits on holding office, shadowing, and so on
Do group members have the procedural skills that they need?	For example, committee skills, education, training, mentoring
Do group members have the skills for involving and supporting people?	What proportion of people have recognisable roles in the group? Is there evidence of motivational leadership, good facilitation, mediation, creative ways of involving people and so on?
Does the group know whether it is being successful?	Are there an effective benchmarking, target-setting and monitoring processes?
Are group members encouraged to move beyond the day-to-day agenda?	Good methods include, visioning sessions, away-days, integrated community planning, mutual aid activities, visits to other places and groups

Notes

11

How do groups ensure that their representatives are accountable?

Explanation

As indicated earlier, representatives are more likely to be accountable if they are delegated from thriving groups and communities who are demanding information and answers to questions. However, there are also a number of procedural factors that can help to strengthen accountability.

Key indicator

Representatives are accountable and have the power to make decisions.

Exercise instructions

This assessment should be made of all of the representatives on the partnership board, not just those of communities.

Table 11   Checklist

Checklist	Explanation
How are representatives selected?	For example, are they self-selected or selected on the basis of their expertise? Are they appointed or elected?
Who do representatives report to?	Is there a formal requirement for them to report back?
What information do they make available to those to whom they are accountable?	For example, does the group have access to all the documents that the representative has, or just a note of decisions taken, *or* nothing at all?
Are representatives briefed and mandated?	Is there a formal process of consultation/ instruction prior to decisions being made? Do representatives have the authority to make autonomous decisions?
Can groups and organisations get independent feedback about the quality of their representatives?	Often the only information people get is from their representatives which makes it hard to judge the quality and impartiality

What provision is there to ensure turnover
of representatives?

It is normally good practice to ensure people are
representatives for a time-limited period?

Notes

Impact assessments

Five

12

How effective is participatory decision making?

Explanation

It is important to check, not only that communities are involved, but that issues of importance to *them* are discussed and that decisions by them are implemented.

Key indicator

(a) Issues of importance to the community get on to agendas.
(b) Decisions made by the community are implemented.

Exercise instructions

The decision trail can be used in two ways. It can start with an item that a local community puts on the partnership agenda which can be tracked through the decision-making process to see whether it gets implemented or blocked. Using a decision trail would be like putting dye in the system and seeing where it flows through and where it gets blocked. A range of partnership decisions should be tested. Their path should be traced back into the partner organisations to see how they have (or have not) been implemented.

Table 12   Impact assessment

Decision trail

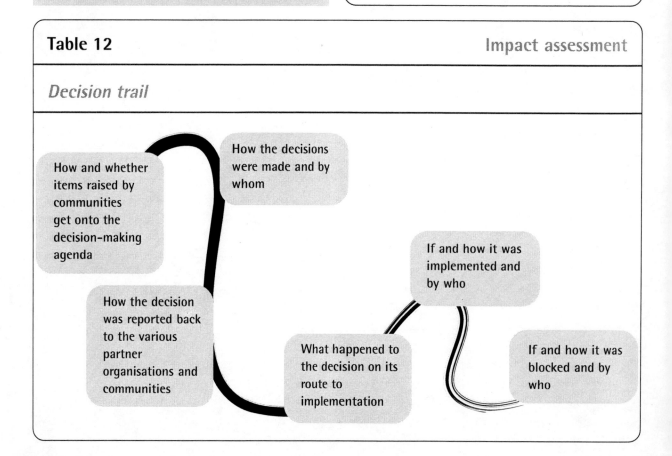

Notes

13

What are the outcomes of participation?

Explanation

It is not enough to establish mechanisms for community participation. It is necessary to establish that they have a tangible impact (although this may not necessarily be measurable).

Key indicator

Outcomes result from participation that would not have happened if participation had not occurred.

Exercise instructions

Answers to the questions below could be ascertained through focus groups and individual questionnaires.

Table 13	Impact assessment
Checklist	**Explanation**
What real differences have resulted from community participation?	What has happened that otherwise would not have happened?
Who has benefited?	This should be assessed with reference to the communities identified in the mapping stage.
Are there examples of problems that have resulted from the community not being listened to?	For example, in one area a community consultation which said that the area could sustain 15 shops was ignored and a whole shopping center was built. Only 15 of the shops in it are still open!
Are there any negative impacts of participation?	Would more have been achieved using another strategy, for example campaigning? Are communities suffering from 'committee overload' etc? Are representatives being incorporated into the system?

Notes

14

Who benefits from participation?

Explanation

It is important to establish whether some communities are more involved than others, and to identify what should be done to change this.

Equally it is necessary to establish whether some groups benefit more than others from their participation.

Key indicator

(a) Opportunities are provided for all sections of the community to participate.
(b) Participation benefits all sections of the community.

Exercise instructions

You should identify *who* is involved in *what* and *how* they have benefitted, or otherwise.

The groups in this table should be the same as those in Table B.

Table 14   Impact assessment

Checklist

Age-based groups

Economic communities

Ethnic and religious communities

Service users

Communities of interest

Communities of identity

Workplace communities

'Outcast' communities

Geographical communities

Sub-communities

Notes

Postscript

The Joseph Rowntree Foundation has provided
funding to roadtest this audit tool, together with a
framework for 'benchmarking community
involvement' devised by COGS. The two
frameworks will be tested over a period of one
year in two Regional Development Agency areas
across a wide range of partnerships. This process
will lead to a refinement of both, and possibly to
the creation of a unified framework.

References and further reading

Arnstein, S.R. (1971) 'A ladder of participation in the USA', *Journal of the Royal Town Planning Institute*, April, pp 176–82.

Atkinson, R. (1999) 'Discourses of partnership and empowerment in contemporary British urban regeneration', *Urban Studies*, vol 36, no 1, pp 59-72.

Barr, A., Hashagan, S. and Purcell, R. (1996a) *Monitoring and evaluation of community development in Northern Ireland: Report*, Belfast: Voluntary Activity Unit.

Barr, A., Hashagan, S. and Purcell, R. (1996b) *Monitoring and evaluation of community development in Northern Ireland: A handbook for practitioners*, Belfast: Voluntary Activity Unit.

Burns, D. and Taylor, M. (1998) *Mutual aid and self-help: Coping strategies for excluded communities*, Bristol/York: The Policy Press/ JRF.

Burns, D., Hambleton, R. and Hoggett, P. (1994) *The politics of decentralisation: Revitalising local democracy*, London: Macmillan.

Beetham, D. (1994) *Defining and measuring democracy*, London: Sage Publications.

Bussmann, W. (1996) 'Democracy and evaluation's contribution to negotiation, empowerment and information', *Evaluation*, vol 2, pp 307–19.

Chanan, G. and West, A. (1999) *Regeneration and sustainable communities*, London: Community Development Foundation.

Clarke (1995) *A missed opportunity: An initial assessment of the 1995 SRB approvals and their impact.*

Clegg, S. (1989) *Framworks of power*, London: Sage Publications.

COGS (2000) *Active partners: Benchmarking community participation in regeneration*, York: Yorkshire Forward.

Connell, P., Kubisch, A., Schorr, L. and Weiss, C. (eds) (1995) *New approaches to evaluating community initiatives: Concepts, methods and contexts*, Washington, DC: The Aspen Institute.

Day, P. and Klein, R. (1987) *Accountabilities: Five public services*, London: Tavistock.

Department of the Environment (1995) *Involving communities in urban and rural regeneration: A guide for practitioners*, London: DoE.

Department of the Environment, Transport and the Regions (1997) *Involving communities in urban and rural regeneration: A guide for practitioners*, London: DETR.

Gaster, L. and Taylor, M. (1993) *Learning from consumers and citizens*, Luton: Local Government Management Board.

Hastings, A., McArthur, A. and McGregor, A. (1996) *Less than equal: Community organisations and estate regeneration partnerships*, Bristol: The Policy Press.

Leat, D. and Taylor, M. (1997) 'Community', *Non-profit Management and Leadership*, vol 7, no 1.

Mawson, J., Beazley, M., Burfitt, A. et al (1995) *The Single Regeneration Budget: The stocktake*, Birmingham: University of Birmingham.

Mayo, E. (1996) *Social auditing for voluntary organisations*, London: Volprof, City University Business School.

Morrissey, J. (2000) 'Indicators of citizen participation: lessons from learning teams in rural EZ/EC communities', *Community Development Journal*, vol 35, no 1, pp 59–74.

Parachini, L., Mott, A. with Rees, S. (1998) 'Strengthening community voices: community-based monitoring, learning and action for an era of devolution', *NFG Reports: Newsletter of the Neighbourhood Funders Group*, vol 5, no 1.

Paton, R. and Foot, J. (1998) 'What do externally accredited standards do for voluntary organisations? Findings from an exploratory study', Paper to the NCVO 'Researching the Voluntary Sector' conference.

Paton, R., Payne, G. and Foot, J. (1998) 'What does "best practise" benchmarking offer non-profits?', Paper presented to the British Academy of Management Conference.

Paton, R. and Foot, J. (1998) 'What do externally accredited standards do for voluntary organisations? Findings from an exploratory study', Paper presented to the NCVO 'Researching the Voluntary Sector' Conference.

Power, M. (1997) *The audit society*, Oxford: Oxford University Press.

Pratt, J., Gordon, P. and Plamping, D. (1999) *Working whole systems*, London: King's Fund.

Rhodes, R. (1995) *The new governance: Governing without government*, Swindon: Economic and Social Research Council.

Rhodes, R. (1997) *Understanding governance: Policy networks, governance, reflexivity and accountability*, Buckingham: Open University Press.

SEU (Social Exclusion Unit) (2000) *National strategy for neighbourhood renewal: A framework for consultation*, London: Cabinet Office.

Smith, M. (1998) *Effective community monitoring of partnerships*.

Stewart, M. and Taylor, M. (1995) *Empowerment and estate regeneration: A critical review*, Bristol: The Policy Press.

Vanderplaat, M. (1995) 'Beyond technique: issues in evaluating for empowerment', *Evaluation*, vol 1, no 1, pp 81–96.

Woolf, E. (1990) *Auditing today*, 4th edn, Englewood Cliffs, NJ: Prentice Hall.

Wales Council for Voluntary Action (1998) *Evaluating community projects for European funding*, Caerphilly: Wales Council for Voluntary Action.